# Rain Inside

## Selected Poems by Ibrahim Nasrallah

### Translated by Omnia Amin and Rick London

a Middlepoint Book
## Curbstone Press

FIRST EDITION, 2009
Copyright ©2009 by Ibrahim Nasrallah
Translation ©2009 by Omnia Amin & Rick London
All Rights Reserved

Cover Design: Susan Shapiro
Cover artwork by Ibrahim Nasrallah
Printed on acid-free paper by Bookmobile

This book was published
with the support of the
National Endowment for
the Arts, the Connecticut
Commission on Culture and
Tourism and donations from
many individuals. We are
very grateful for this support.

Connecticut Commission
on Culture & Tourism

Library of Congress Cataloging-in-Publication Data

Nasr Allah, Ibrahim.
  [Matar fi al-dakhil. English]
  Rain inside : selected poems / by Ibrahim Nasrallah ; translated by
Omnia Amin and Rick London. -- 1st ed.
    p. cm.
  ISBN 978-1-931896-52-8 (pbk. : alk. paper)
  I. Amin, Omnia. II. London, Rick. III. Title.

PJ7852.A688M3813 2009
892'.716--dc22

                                    2009010064

CURBSTONE PRESS   321 Jackson Street   Willimantic, CT 06226
       phone: 860-423-5110   e-mail: info@curbstone.org
                       www.curbstone.org

# Acknowledgments

The translators thank Mona Darwazah, Ibrahim Nasrallah's wife, for her insight, continued support, encouragement, and friendship, without which we would not have this translation of Nasrallah's poetry. We also thank Anthony Thompson and Scott Sutton for their incisive suggestions. And our deepest gratitude goes to Dr. Peter Stromberg for his close reading of the entire work and invaluable suggestions throughout.

# Table of Contents

# Ibrahim Nasrallah

## A Replenishing Poet of the Diaspora

**By Dr. Omnia Amin**

### 1. Verbal Weapons

On coming to introduce Ibrahim Nasrallah to Western readers, I wanted to simply say that Nasrallah is a Palestinian poet. For an Arabic speaking audience, that statement is enough to suggest much of what characterizes his poetry, but I discovered that it means very little to Western readers. This led me to think of how to differentiate for English readers a Palestinian poet from other Arab poets. Is there indeed a difference? Isn't Arabic poetry all one and the same? And if not, then how does Palestinian poetry differ from the rest of the poetry of the Arab world?

Palestinian poetry is no doubt a part of Arabic poetry. What distinguishes it from the rest of Arabic poetry is the historical and political background of what the Palestinians underwent as a nation for what is known as the "Palestinian Cause." Since 1878, when the first Zionist colony was founded near Jaffa, the Palestinians have faced more than a century of struggle to free their occupied land, and to preserve their identity as a race and a people. As more Jewish settlers flocked in from around the world, the struggle of the Palestinian people intensified, complicated by their being under the colonial rule of the British Empire. A point of crisis in this struggle came in 1917 with the Balfour Declaration, as Arthur James Balfour, British Secretary of State for Foreign Affairs, promised a national home for Jews in Palestine. What followed was a series of defeats among Palestinians attempting to protect their land, until events culminated in the 1948 war between Palestinians and Zionists. Palestinians, being ill-organized and poorly armed, were defeated, and an independent Jewish State was proclaimed in Tel Aviv. The events of 1948 are referred to by Palestinians and Arabs as "The Catastrophe." Since that time, Palestinians have been struggling for self rule and national recognition, especially as the dominance of Israeli forces, and the historic massacres that took place, led to the Palestinian Diaspora. Since 1948, many Palestinians have lived in refugee camps in Jordan and Lebanon, and the situation for Palestinians has only gotten worse. Having lost most of their land, they are now confined to the Gaza Strip and the West Bank, or to exile in different parts of the world. The State of Israel today is internationally recognized and the Palestinian people are fighting not only for a homeland, but for commensurate international recognition. In their bitter fight for their rights, they have come to be labeled as terrorists, and any initiative on their part is subject to interpretation as terrorist activity.

Palestinian poets today write under the influence of this historical, political, social and psychological background. The preponderance of their poetry, especially that written in the modern era after 1948, is usually termed the "Poetry of Resistance." Through the act of writing, Palestinian poets have attempted to assert their identity and draw attention to the struggles and sorrows of their people, and at the same time provide a unified voice for a population scattered among many countries. Poetry became an integral part of the commitment to the Palestinian Cause, as it formed into a verbal weapon for all Palestinians, whether in their homeland, treated as second class citizens, or in exile. So when a Palestinian poet writes about sustained suffering and loss of identity and belonging it means more than when the issue is addressed by a poet of any other Arab nationality. Their words resonate in the consciousness and conscience of the Arab nation, as they mark the ongoing sorrow and suffering of the Palestinian people.

## 2. A Collective Voice

With a spirit of commitment, of faith in the self, and a refusal to accept repression and national dispossession, Nasrallah and many poets of his generation delineate their experience in a voice that is as much personal as it is collective. They render the great collective consciousness of their people who bravely face suffering on so many levels. Being under a constant state of siege and an ongoing condition of exile has created a profound crisis of identity, as some Palestinians are denied even the simple right to a passport, and have to live their lives away from their ancestral homeland. This means that a Palestinian poetry implies both poetry written by Palestinians who are living in their country, and that of Palestinian writers living in the Diaspora.

Nasrallah is one of the exiled Palestinian poets who lives permanently in Jordan, away from his parents' homeland. He does not fall neatly into the group of poets who call themselves Poets of Resistance, as his poetry transcends any determination of personal strife, reaching to universal themes, where the sorrows of all humanity are realized. He is among the foremost avant-garde poets of his generation, affirming the strength and perseverance of his people, but also the universality of defiance of any form of injustice against mankind. His courage has cost him a great deal. More than any other modern Arab poet, Nasrallah's works have been banned, and he has been prevented from reading his poetry in official public venues.

As far back as 1985, Nasrallah, was denied travel for political reasons. He wrote poems and songs for the musical group "Baladna." The 45 songs he composed for the group made up most of the material they sang and the performance of the songs left a great mark on the cultural scene in Jordan, among a wide range of audiences. His popular success, and the nature of his writing, that stirs the dormant dreams of his people, resulted in his being denied travel for six years, during which time he was not allowed to read publicly. In 1996, his novel *Birds of Caution* was published, and instantly confiscated. The novel presented a bold vision of the events revolving around Black September of 1970, and the novel was allowed to be distributed only after a far-reaching campaign was undertaken by writers in Jordan and the Arab world. In 1999, his poetry collection *In the Name of the Mother and Son* was published, and was subsequently bitterly defamed. Nasrallah was labeled a heretic because of this collection, which told the story of the life of his mother and her relationship with his father in 33 poems. The situation threatened harsh damage to his personal reputation, but the press and cultural institutions stood beside him, and helped him to overcome these accusations.

In 2006, in an unprecedented action, his collected poems were put in the custody of the Attorney General. This was the first time that a literary work was handed over to the court by the state. The state persisted in its decision and refused to withdraw the case from the Attorney General's office, even after the protests of the Writers' Association. The situation grew in notoriety and a number of international and Arab cultural institutions intervened on Nasrallah's behalf, as well many individual poets and writers around the world. Under the growing threat of a scandal, the government withdrew its case. The government's condemnation had been related to a passage that narrated a love story between a Palestinian Moslem warrior and a Jordanian Christian woman. It was a bold assertion of artistic freedom and a refusal of any form of discrimination or sectarianism.

Today, Nasrallah does not face such direct confrontations, but since the early 90's he has been prohibited from giving talks or readings at Jordan's state run universities. The last time he appeared on Jordanian television was in 1982.

The above events have only compelled Nasrallah to work harder. He describes his experience of writing poetry by saying: "I rush through life chasing one question after another, searching for an answer whereby I can rest a little, before I run once more after the rest of the questions." He believes that "nothing is ever complete inside us, as we are inexhaustible." Poetry for him is a quest for the meaning of life, of existence, offering a unique moment to understand the self. He says: "Writing is our best opportunity to understand ourselves clearly; therefore, the secret of writing resides in the fact that we become whole in the act of writing, unlike any other moment in life." In writing, he sees the human being fully awakened, with all of his senses and metaphysical endowments. Writing affords him an affinity with the whole of humanity, with the whole of nature, and with all times. It is this vision, along with his inclination to use words in their simplest form to illustrate the most complex of human experiences, that makes him unique among poets of his generation. His popular readings demonstrate his feelings of oneness with his audience and the universal element of his poetry welcomes translation. And in this sense, the success that Nasrallah has had as a writer and a person comes from the open and sincere way he engages others. His background, and his transformation of it, allows him to connect deeply with people and to remain in their hearts and memories.

## 3. A Simple Background

There is nothing in Nasrallah's background that would foretell the birth of a poet whose writing would embrace a distinctively universal element. He was born in Amman, Jordan, in 1954, under humble circumstances. His parents, both illiterate, came from Al Breuij, a small village near Jerusalem. They were forced to leave their home and take refuge at the Al Wehdat refugee camp in Jordan, as a result of Israeli occupation. Nasrallah grew up in the refugee camp, spending the first thirty-three years of his life there. He attended school at the United Nation's Relief and Works Agency for Palestinian Refugees (UNRWA), and later studied at the UNRWA Teachers Training College in Amman. After graduating from college, he worked for two years in the Qunfudah region of Saudi Arabia, teaching Arabic to school children. It was an experience that he turned into his first novel, *Prairies of Fever*, published in 1985. Nasrallah worked as a journalist from 1978 till 1996. In 1996, he became the director of cultural affairs at Darat Al Funun (Home of the Arts), becoming vice president of the cultural and literary department in 2002.

Nasrallah started writing at a young age. His first attempts to express himself in poetry were the result of painful events. When he was in the ninth grade his Arabic teacher at school, who lived fifty meters away from him, was killed by a bomb explosion, and his body was scattered all over his yard. Nasrallah dedicated his first written lines to him in an elegy that has been followed by many more attempts to give expression to a world where life and death, beauty and horror, love and hate, coexist. From that moment Nasrallah began his life as a poet: "I started writing then and I continue to write today, as I believe that everything can be turned into poetry. I believe that everything lies here inside this seventh continent I call the human being, before it comes to be anywhere outside."

His first collection of poems, *Horses Overlooking the City*, appeared in 1980, and soon after it was published he became a celebrated poet. He has been awarded prestigious prizes for his poetry: The Jordanian Writers' Association Award for the best volume of poetry for the years 1980, 1982, and 1984; The Arar Literary Award for Jordanian and Arab poets in 1991; and The Al Uwais Literary Award for Arab poetry by the UAE in 1997.

After years of writing poetry, Nasrallah undertook to write his first novel, commenting: "I truly believe that a human being cannot express himself in only one way throughout his entire life." He has now written ten novels, in addition to numerous articles on literature, poetry, and the film arts. He has continued to express himself even more broadly in art. Today, he is also known as a painter and photographer. He has participated in several exhibitions, and his first solo photography exhibition, *The Autobiography of An Eye*, was held at Darat Al Funun, in Jordan, in 1995, followed by *Under Two Suns: Images and Words,* in 2004. In the same year, he also participated in the Fifth Gwangju Biennale, in South Korea.

### 4. A Man of Many Talents

Being a man of many artistic talents lends Nasrallah's

poetry a rich flavor. He is sensitive to the minute details and the delicate fleeting moments of life that a painter's or a photographer's eye is quick to catch. His poetry, laden with images, achieves great drama, despite the simplicity of his style, because of his nostalgia for his ancestors' hometown and his own sense of being uprooted from it. Through his poetry, he is able to create enough space to transcend what another writer might simply record as a morbid experience. He finds that core of individual identity that ironically comes from a sense of belonging to the whole of the human race. The sorrow of the Palestinian people and their struggles become integrated within the larger frame of life and existence as Nasrallah locates the complicated reality of the individual human life within a larger philosophical and existential awareness. He sees into life with the eye of an artist, and with a natural human tendency toward a love that can heal, transcend, and transform the pain and sorrow of human experience.

Selected by Nasrallah, the poems in this book come from several collections. Nasrallah is well known in the Arab world for his short poems that resemble the Japanese Haiku, as they work on awakening philosophical insight by means of an everyday event or object. This book also presents a selection of his medium-length poems that honor and transcend the Palestinian experience by opening it onto the world, and by opening his poems to the pain of every individual who lives in difficulty, without regard to color, religion, or national identity.

*Rain Inside* holds before us the painful events of our shared human history, events that must never be hidden or forgotten, since they are being reenacted in today's world. And yet this work is about transforming the tears shed in anguish and moments of despair into a replenishing rain inside the human self. Or, in Nasrallah's own words: "I see writing like a river that flows on earth and rises to the sky. It covers vast distances until it softens and slows or madly rushes on in bends or over mighty waterfalls. It is the river that always tells me: Be different and be yourself! It is the river that tells me: Use me for your compass, for I will always find my direction."

# RAIN INSIDE

# The Windows

Windows are a first step into the world,
a song on a spacious cloud,
a departure, a rose,
the braids of the moon falling over hills,
a heartbeat in the darkness of the night
that travels in chains
and in men.
They are a threshold for the prayers
of our lonely neighbor,
an oasis for lovers
and children, the tempting fruit
in baskets, the seagull in the heart
bent down in sleep, the wisdom of the walls
arising from silent rocks and moving
toward mountaintops.

# Devilishness

It appeals to us to summon the streets like a herd of wild goats
and shepherd them to the plains
with a staff made for sweet commotion.
It appeals to us to reach out and pluck a star
and with it to joyously ornament a slender lady.
It appeals to us to elude our watches, jobs, wives,
and the cycle of time and silence.
It appeals to us to shake our bodies and our muteness,
to send a thousand emissaries to love.
It appeals to us to fold up our souls
and plunge into the lute's song,
into what a forest tells us
and what drums say.
It appeals to us to hold a woman by her waist at the end of
                                                    the night
and beguile the roses till they happily confess their dew
and their seasons.
It appeals to us to take hold of a withered branch
to consummate a marriage.
It appeals to us to see what's there to see,
to see it and to speak.
It appeals to us to become young again,
to witness our birth in the fields.
It appeals to us to safeguard our children with lilies,
not with spears or blades.
It appeals to us to sing out:
It is appealing!
It is appealing to take our leave and go downtown—

but the cities are closed down.
Their sun has been guillotined
and their smiles are muddy with blood.

# Our Songs

Who are these songs for?
When they break the silence of the night
spreading warmth and life over the snow,
when they fall on the jasmine and carry it to water,
when they pass by a dim window, secretly embracing a lover,
when they spread over the grass, wrapped in clouds?
Who are these songs for
when they free the flowers
and the hidden flame of passion in women,
when they come to you with their flowers,
when they come to me with their secrets,
when they embrace the sun or a bouquet of flowers
or anything abandoned on the road?
When they send a pulse into the ground
and the pulse blossoms into a flower
in the space between two deaths,
or in a cloud, or in fire?
Who are these songs for
when they laugh,
who are these songs for
when they rise?
And who are these songs for
when they open the doors of our houses
and embrace us one by one,
returning us to our lore?
When they carry our bodies in weddings
and cushion us with a lovely homeland
and then pick the most delicious fruit
and the farthest star
and hide them from the eyes of soldiers
to carry them—like our mother—home to us?

# Beginnings

When all the birds in the world flap their wings in unison
as one body, when the waters of springs and mountain streams
gather in a dusty palm,
when a human being runs
and trees and the hidden future follow him,
when the world becomes simple
and I can climb onto a table in the office of the daily news
and speak of your love to the elegant shuttered windows,
to the good and bad paintings on the walls,
when I am able to freely place a gentle kiss
on your cheek in public,
when I am able to return with you after midnight
without a police patrol desecrating our bodies
in search of a confession,
when we can run in the streets
without anyone pronouncing us crazy,
when I am able to sing
and share a stranger's umbrella
and when she in turn may share my loaf of bread,
when you are able to say I love you
without fear of death or imprisonment
and I can open a window in the morning
without being silenced by a bullet,
when I am able to grow older
and the trees are added to your attire
and we can count the drops of rain on each other's faces
and can sing and love free of weapons,
raids, chronic fear, and disappearances—
another world will begin,

a new homeland will have been readied.
But for now we announce a new beginning with our death,
a new beginning of love.

# Steps

Have you noticed?
You cross the earth with your steps and your singing,
leaving for a faraway place
after years that have seemed as tired as the houses
but as free as the clouds
as the vehicles of the wind quit pounding the days
and you depart with them
as they shake the dust from their invisible bodies
and fling their bridles at words, shadows and wooden benches.
Have you noticed?
You slip away with your dreams, your blood,
with horses, heights, water, sky,
cars, boats, and trains.
You've run away.
Have you noticed?
After all this
the earth is still wider than the ways of
your narrowing steps,
your short wings,
and your singing is barely complete.

## Prayer

Farah, we will begin our prayers
amid this bloody sorrow
and among the lonely pine.
What makes the mountains this morning much kinder,
the sun more glamorous,
the wind a song that celebrates the heights?
What makes our beloved jasmine
more pure than we imagined
and more disobedient than we had thought?
What makes these mountains
and these trees that we allowed to be taller than us
much shorter than us now?
Farah, we will continue our prayers
and conjure new seasons for our lives,
new rivers to flow in our veins
and a new place for the world's singing.
We will continue our prayers
and when love is total,
when our fingers shyly and tenderly come together
like beads of the fig's milk,
we will climb the mountain to bless all creatures
and together whisper: Amen … amen.

# Birth

The woman who gives birth to us
after the trees possess our bodies
and bend with weariness,
after summer surprises us
with frost and darkness—
the woman who gives birth to us
after fruits become inaccessible
and happiness becomes a cruel star,
after our waters dry up
and our green seems more sorrowful
than on any other day—
the woman who gives birth to us
after travel dwells in us
and boats forget us,
after we're stranded on the quays of ports and of life,
on the aircraft of a stone age—
the woman who gives birth to us
after songs go round
and cause our eyes to tremble with pain,
after their wings become still
or their absence fills us—
the woman who gives birth to us
after we lose patience
and cannot be contained:
We will cry on her doorstep in the fever of a second birth.
We will cry and shout:
No to all women and cities that fill us with false pride.
We will cry and bid them,
and all cruel stones,
and the perfection of wax,
farewell.

## The Wings

Whenever I catch a poem
I've caught a wing that takes me to the steady radiance
at the heart of the world, to the lifeblood
in the veins of all creatures.
I know now that happiness has more than one wing
and so tonight I will cross the city with my little bit of money,
with fingers that know only poems,
in search of a harp.
And I will cross the city seeking a wing
and in the morning when the sun rises,
and the world seems bigger than words,
bigger than the threads that songs
and dewy lamps overshadow,
I will search for colors
and buy paper and a paintbrush
to seek out another wing.
But what pains me is that this body slowly stiffens,
that one day I will not be able to dance ballet:
a happiness that hovers with a thousand wings.

# Exposition

What does a lover want from a bird on its perch
clutching shivers of sunlight and trees in its claws like dreams?
What do human beings want?
Do they want it to sleep in their palm?
To delight in tranquility?
To twist itself around and walk on its wings?
To knock at the door and take a seat like an obedient boy
who washes his soul in the sink?
What do they want?
Do they want it to bring reassuring headlines?
To sweep boredom away from their lives?
To be a witty companion, or a guillotine for loneliness?
What do they want?
Do they want it to gracefully climb stairs,
walk on a tightrope like an acrobat,
gather its dreams,
hammer its past, cook songs
and swallow the withering silence?
What do they want?
Do they want it to sit in the evening
telling stories that put the heart and the whole family to sleep?
What do they want?
Do they want it to silently bend down at night's end
and beat its beak with its wings
striving to answer the human questions?
What do they want?
What do they want?
Do you want more
than its morning surprise
as it fills the soul with its song?

# Joy

In the pathways and rest stops of your smooth palm,
when we joyfully go out for a day forgetting our umbrella
and miss the summer as a passing cloud surprises us,
when you are caught between lightly falling rain and me,
you run here, you laugh there.
The clouds disappear from your face,
amazed like all the trees in all of the houses.
And you smile and say: We forgot the umbrella.
I see in you the joy of a dream.
You become kinder than a curved wooden peg,
wider than a wish,
bigger than a proper lady.
You become a child!

# Frost

He is shivering.
He stands close to the fire,
warming his arteries, his heart
near the stove.
He shivers.
—*O my friend,*
*did you ever wrap yourself in a winter's night*
*and wake up alone on a frozen midnight bench*
*naked and uncovered?*
I said: *It must be a dream then.*
He said:
*No, my friend, it is parting with a woman*

≈ ≈ ≈

He is shivering.
Winter is far away.
July is not yet over.
He leaned toward me and gave me his hand,
then talked with me for two nights.
We walked the distance from the city till dawn
in two moments, in two glasses.
He dispelled his virgin sorrows
and sipped two tears.

≈ ≈ ≈

The wind blows in his heart
so the north winds fill with frost.

*—O my friend,*
*did you bundle up in a winter coat*
*when you reached the middle of the road*
*and hills of snow slept on your shoulders*
*and when you touched your body*
*were you lonely like my heart?*
I said: *It must be a dream then.*
He said: *My friend, it is a long goodbye.*

≈ ≈ ≈

He was shivering.
He leaves for the east in the morning
and for the west in the evening
and comes to me when midnight
is a lifetime frozen in his lungs.
I hand him a cup of tea and as he laughs
I hear his sides splitting.
*—O my friend, will tea help?*

He leaned toward my heart
and sang a lot.
I asked: *Singing helps?*
He said: *A little.*

And he sang a lot.

## His Shadow is Departing

He sips her face in the winter morning,
descends the stairs of her sorrows
and sings of warmth.
A path opens before him and he takes it.

≈ ≈ ≈

On the road a woman hands him morning coffee.
He drinks to sad eyes somewhere far away
and takes shelter on the horizon for two years,
then moves on leaving behind the warm coffee.

≈ ≈ ≈

His shadow travels
while the evenings revolve
to take the shape of a woman's lips.
Her sorrow envelops him like air.
He tries on her face on the night train
and searches for her in newspapers.
He bleeds.
She is never present
in anything that describes her!

≈ ≈ ≈

In the street he finds a path through his sorrows
and searches for her.
Life passes

and nothing on earth can
hold his ribs together again.

≈ ≈ ≈

Today a thousand paths branch out from his sorrow
and merge in the cold where footsteps freeze.
He smiles at a passerby on the road
who befriends him for one night, two nights.
She toys with his sorrows, then leaves,
leaving him bare as autumn,
without green,
without shoulders.

≈ ≈ ≈

Life surges right before his eyes
and deserts creep toward him.
He takes cover behind his ribs
as the trees are too distant to hold back the sand
or bring on a light rain.

≈ ≈ ≈

He wanders through all the cafés on the street
and a thousand women invite him to dance.
He sees her and follows her in all of these women
and when he is alone he adds
a thousand new names and a quenched experience
to his sorrows.

≈ ≈ ≈

18

Her face is now more intimate to him
than the palm of his hand.
When she covers his nakedness in the streets
he will swear before joining with her that the eyes
that turned away from him on the shore
will greet him again.
He digs in the sand, buries his sorrows, and walks away.

≈ ≈ ≈

In the beautiful morning
he feels the grass on the surface of the sand
as it spreads and spreads
until it grows over his forearms and his shoulders
and the silent moment between imagination
and what the eyes see.
He mutters a morning greeting to himself, as is his habit,
but …
A woman answers.

≈ ≈ ≈

He drowns time in memory,
gathers up a bundle of light
and walks to the river.
She bares her wound
to be with him.

≈ ≈ ≈

…Winter, spring, and summer,

but autumn is near.
He sips her features
and takes on her wounds…
autumn is far away.

# A Wish

What would happen if the moon came down to us
and rested in our arms?
If flowers were our streets and our poems?
If the sun became our secret?
If our fingers ignited the wisdom
in an old man's heart
and his many locked up secrets
lit up our own hearts?
If a woman lit our souls on a cold day
as she passed by us?
If only by chance
she would pass by!

## I Am the Wind

I know that I will labor on and on without rest.
I will not stop dancing because I'm
more beautiful than the murderers and the slain.
I know that I scatter my body
and the flowers of my soul
so as never to be seen in a tomb.
I know I will wake again and again.
But when the wind tires will there be a hill
where it may lay its head to rest?
For I am the wind.

# The Last Supper

I am calling you—so come in your white dress
that brushes softly on the pavement, with that dream
in your eyes.
I call your horses, rivers, flying fish,
and the balconies that did not look down on us,
scattering their flowers.
I call upon friends who have defiled our poems
and the trails of jasmine inside us,
I call birds that have kept their weddings from us
and the wind that has knifed its horses.
I remember the streets,
the light taking shelter in a woman's bosom,
the roof overhead rising with a flock of pigeons.
I call the now deserted city
where I hid among the crowd.
I call the beautiful one who hovers around these houses
and the one who died, my dear lady,
and the one who does not die.
I call your predatory birds,
wreaths, graves and departures.
There you are
and there they are
and here I am.
We are no longer birds in the sky
so let us eat our own wings.

# Evasion

You didn't know that songs go round
and return home to find only my heart.
You didn't know that birds sing
and when night falls they perch sadly on my arm.
By the end of the night they know my secret.
You didn't know that I gather up the fields
whose trees rise from the earth
and run like small children.
They sleep nearby and wake in the morning
and steal my poetry.
You didn't know that my soul swells
like an expanse between my ebb and flow,
that at night's end I'm overtaken
by deadly joy and wanton weariness—
so my song and my wine get intoxicated.
You didn't know that I'm sharp as a wing,
as a song silently astray, that since I came to this wide world
I've lived here and there avoiding this dark age.
You didn't know that I disappear like an echo
and abide like a shadow
now spreading to escape the grave.

# Evasion (2)

I prepare a thousand horses for you, a thousand causes
to greet you on a Sunday evening.
I count suns for lips that have awakened desire
and ripened grapes and led flowers from gardens
to the deserts of the body.
I plan my day: I lead a herd of clouds to you
gently leaving them to remove foam
from the soul and the eclipse of our weddings.
I ready a canopy for you and a bed
and two brown arms and a flame and a wedding ring
and a group of disobedient boys,
so I may stay away.

# Defiance

His mother will pull him away from useless trouble,
from birds taking the morning into arbors of vine
and bitter grapes
and fields of long-necked wheat.
She will pull him away from the almond tree
and the wall
and the wind
and the irksome morning rooster
that chafes the backs of chickens
and the silence of the courtyard.
She will take him away and whisper:
*I won't be late, now be an angel,*
and she gorgeously goes out and locks the door behind her.
Alone, he contemplates his surroundings:
a mulberry tree, a dusty cat, ashes, mud on the road,
water gurgling on the doorstep, the winter season
not yet begun, fire at the hoof of a tethered horse,
a storm stirring in the night dance of a gypsy,
the chaos of the Khamasin winds as they rip tents from
the ground
and scatter Bedouins across their desert.
—*Be an angel,* she told him.
He laughs.
Mother is crazy!
How could I?
He breaks the lock and darts across the alley.
He runs and runs.
I will explain to her and she will forgive me:
*Mother, if I became an angel,*
*I would burden your heart even more.*

He runs and runs.
Mud covers everything.
He runs and soon the angel's white garments are smeared
                                                    with mud.

He runs and runs and runs.

# Defiance (2)

Rebelling against the teachings in books,
against a long ribbon of commandments and wooden songs,
against my father's shadow, against lessons in mathematics
and disasters told to a flute—about a blueness swallowed
                                             by clouds,
about an appointment kept by indolence,
about the verdant shadows of embers,
about braids fastened by iron, about a knifing, about a jar
that springs from the flaccid moon,
about visions yawning in a passageway,
about chained horses and gypsies who trade their sun for gold.
Rebelling till there's no difference between one who falls
and one who leaps.
Our school benches have deceived us.
Hell is no longer Hell and Heaven is not Heaven, except in books.
I will scream like a wounded ibex in the path of a bullet—
whose steps are filled with fear
by missiles and thunder.
I will scream at the wind like branches robbed of their soul by fire,
like swords hidden in silk
and songs hidden in rapture.
I will leave to do battle with my soul,
to throw it amid sins prepared for the pious...
here a general and a god will revel in them ...
I will live here with all my sins
and like impetuous fire will begin to play.
I will wade through my earthly heaven
and run in its streets and cry out:
O philanthropists, for God's sake, give me one sin.
Give me one sin!

# Rushing

I will open my window in the morning
and recite the poem before letting it go its way
like the song of a bird,
like the sun at the start of its journey,
like a wave hitting rock
or the heart slipping from a lover's breast,
I will reach like a branch
drawn by the green of a wild spring
beheld by a young woman.
I will tire and slump down but there will be no shade for me,
except the shadow of a wing.
There's no earth for me except for what my hand
can grab from the expanse.
I will sing a lot, will punctuate my song with happiness
and once more piece together my ribs
and the residue of an echo
and start walking again ...
I surge as if I were the darkness, the mud,
as if I were a long alley that moves in the long night.
I leap like a tiger of the tropics into sleep.
I open my window and my veins and drink songs,
for wine has made my drinking partners swoon.
I become the cold at the bottom of a cup.
I am the cold at the bottom of a cup
and I will run and run, leaving hills of ice behind me.
I will cross the plains and dance waking up a thousand gardens.
And I will follow the tracks of my soul to a faraway place,
to the soul's end, to truth...

# Chase

The wind chases me along passageways,
beleaguers my steps in alleys and across the sky.
The splashing foam chases me across the mountains,
between the vineyard and the greenness of the almond,
in ignited embers, in the joy of chestnuts.
Snow chases me between poems
and in the arms of a lady who inhabited my body
and then buried it in dust
so the birds of annihilation wouldn't see me.
The desert chases my blood for drink
and the inspectors chase me
to plant their imperfections in the space of my heart,
to share my sun and my singing.
Sand chases me and becomes a wall
that sees its dreams in my quietude.
What lies behind me chases me as I hurry along,
and the bellowing evenings chase me.
The paint on the walls in the hallways
decorated with the horns of antelopes chases me.
The tenacious youth chase me with their innocence and
the sobriety of their laughter.
The coldness brimming in the conversation of women chases me,
their whoredom arcing over their carefree beds.
The cycle of time chases me in the corpses of dead friends
and a corpse urges me toward death,
invading my roguish ways and my openness
to dwell in me—
as it withers away the garments of the wise!

## A Special Invitation

My corpse hovered over a sea of silence.
My house was a cloud of dust,
the streets were a wild extinguishing dream
and the night was like the face of a friend divided
between silence and earning one's keep.
The trees opposed their own colors
and the wind opposed riding a song,
a bird in the air was a period
then a comma in conversation.
The sky was arid.
After being killed I washed by the river
and the green along its banks
and when the mourners were late
I rushed to a wave in my mind and plucked a song.
I sang it for two whole nights until it waned
and broke like a mast.
When they were late
I turned onto every path to darkness,
like the soul breaking over the rims of flowers and wooden cups
and said: *They will catch up with me on the way.*
The road was lonesome and the moon ripped apart my body
although this was not the Age of War.

≈ ≈ ≈

My funeral proceeds on its own
moved by the power of darkness to the grave site.
I heard him ask: *Where are they?*
I recognized him by his clothes, his fear, his blue face,
the blood on the collar of his shirt,

by the bullets embedded in his flesh.
I recognized him, I did.
But the mourners were late.
So I said: *Invite my killer*...

# What Julius Caesar Didn't Say

Good evening, my friends.
In a few minutes I'll pull back the cloak
of darkness and cross over into night.
In a few minutes I will go home
to search for what remains of yesterday,
for what collects my soul—and to forget
your familiar faces and vanquish death
with sleep.
In a few minutes I'll go home
and sleep there like the solitary cold.
We have crossed a long night to reach midnight.
So, good evening.
We have read a lot of poetry, until
we extinguished our flame,
and we drank a lot, enough
to return us to our beginnings
in grapes and dust.
Every jugular has been lifted up and expanded,
laying each of us out like an open book
before his own eyes.
Good evening, my friends.
Soon I will take my songs from your day
and move in the night's darkness
nearer to my blood to regain my bearings.
Never mind, my friends.
Don't listen to me.
We've drunk a lot.
We are too tired.
Our souls have shown their coals.
And mystery has given up a few of its secrets.

Now, here I am—regarding your hands and eyes
and wondering what daggers your fingers
ready for me.
My friends ... there is a voice inside me
that cuts through my blood and cries out:
Who will follow me home on this night?
My friends, who among you is my killer?
Who among you is my killer?

# Rain Inside

*(To a man in front of the Scheherazade Café:*
*passed by many … but seen by few)*

Winter pours its rains and winds
over his shoulders.
A dream has its own inclinations.
By using simple words and speaking about the weather
I became familiar with his features.
He silently browses through a book of clouds
and reads the heavy day,
then sears me with his gaze.
I say: *Life is running across the sky and the pavement,*
as he hands me the daily paper.
Water blurs the lines
and burdens sleep.
He whispers: *Never mind.*
Here one becomes familiar with the look of sorrow on the faces,
the whirl of time,
the incantation of silence,
the closed roads.
When I stretched out my hand to him
he became perplexed.
He shook my hand with his left hand
and hid his tears, his pain,
his wooden arm.

≈ ≈ ≈

Birds do not shelter in newspapers.
Tobacco doesn't fill the blood with warmth,

there's only the smoke that comes out of a fearful body.
I say to a tomorrow that never comes,
to stormy rain and an evident torture:
*Life is running across the sky and across the pavement.*
*—We agree then!*
We did not disagree.
The wind swept through his naked cells and a storm exploded.
He was scattered between the buildings and the cold season.
With a shivering arm he sold his papers.

≈ ≈ ≈

Autumn has a hidden storm.
Winter has tinted clouds.
Spring has rushing blood.
Summer has an ember.
A stone has discovered the pain behind his sad eyes,
but the epithets have not yet discovered his secret!
I said to him one morning
—I did not say—
for details are now accumulating between us—
*a corpse ... a stab*
*a stab ... a corpse,*
*and the streets are in our blood.*

I said to him one morning
—I did not say—
*we are the warmth of these streets, their oven in winter.*
*We are clouds that rise*
*from the earth's soil toward the sky.*

I said to him one morning
—I did not say—
…but today when I bid him farewell
he waved back with his wooden arm
and a tremendous joy flooded us
in a homeland of friendship.

# Departure

He did not tell the flowers that gathered along the way:
*Goodbye.*
He did not tell the morning that passes by the earth:
*My friend, I will always be here.*
He did not tell the streets:
*These are my footsteps returning, as is their habit,*
*for these walks help maintain your flavor.*
He did not tell his friend:
*Wait for me.*
He did not tell the young ones:
*I used to play here ... where I grew up,*
*so watch over the playgrounds and the sand until I return.*
He did not tell the city:
*My blood is flowing out of your hands,*
*crossing the sorrows and borders of your neglect.*
He didn't say anything.
He did not gather up the sun, the grapevine, the wounds,
                                        or happiness.
He did not invent a word for departure
and did not shed a faint star in his tears,
nor did he carry grass in his hands, or the rushing trees.
Nor did he spread out his lean fingers in the evening
to collect letters, songs, and some pictures.
He did not say anything.
But when I embraced him ...
he broke in my arms.

# The Exile

Silence becomes solid in bones,
in a bird's song,
in the meaning of a word,
spreading over all of the greenery
and swallowing up the town squares,
creeping like a desert snake
and dwindling the horses' neighing.
Blossoming in my woman's embrace,
in the song's pale light
and in the flowers on balconies,
I gather myself to lift dry clouds from my body
and prayers from my soul.
I see God's sun, my face, and my hand: three doves.
The time that's passed is more than age can carry
and my undulations are in restraints.
The spikes of my soul do not reach the horse's back,
an angle overlaps another angle ... within an angle,
this body of mine.
Poets surround me like the fruit of regret.
My mother says: *White is laughter's waterfall.*
So we laugh till our blood explodes.
Fear encloses the sweet basil and the alley's mint.
My love's touch on my forehead is like a runaway train.
The wind on my shoulders is like a dead horse,
the sea is far away.
Time is a coffin, while nakedness is the daily news.
For thirty three years
I have been digging tunnels
so I might emerge from this cold womb...

## The Wave

You rise up high upon the shore
and the sea becomes a bed of agitated wings.
You rise up high
and my blood flares, my ribs jump, my voice trembles
and horses neigh inside me.
You rise up high.
A secret calling spills into my soul.
As I follow it, I'm overtaken
by the water's swells.
The steps of unnamed wanderers intersect on the sand.
Shells become the wind's lungs and the feathers of dumb birds.
You rise up high
as if the earth's bearings are there inside you,
as if you were my soul transfiguring, my childish bewilderment,
as if you were more than the shore,
more than the sea,
the sun of obscure things.
The steps of unnamed wanderers intersect on the sand.
You rise up high
and we become familiar in the moment
when you stretch your hand toward me
and a blueness spreads in longing.
My heart's hunger brightens for deserted weddings,
for wheat, for martyrs' faces.
I call out to you: *Mother.*
I call out again
and the thirsty antelope of the world rush inside me.
I run toward you,
I run,
I run like an arrow shot out of a dismembered corpse.

# The Returnee

Every day the emigrant comes home from death
to the shadows of his walls,
to his reading lessons,
he crawls to the shadows to rest under the quiet cinchona.

The emigrant comes home from death
to draw out breath from the chain of stone around his house,
from his milk-white feet,
from the rattling air.
He knows the trees,
the angles of the old houses,
the sound of his mother's footsteps in the backyard,
the stories his great grandmother tells to put the mischievous
                                              young ones to sleep.
She plucks night stars as she wishes, after they have entered sleep.

He passes by like a stranger
though he doesn't resemble a stranger in any way.
The people he sees standing now at his door
are the strangers...

## The Stranger

Child,
so many hands broke the bird's wings inside you,
so many bullets are scattered inside you,
so many friends saw wisdom in the sadness of your letters.
So they made up an excuse to leave.
Everything that resembles the soul resembles us.
Is there a difference to tell
between a soul and a wound to the body?
At an early age you were singed with gray hair
and you learned that the world is a conversation
and you put up your tent at the earth's end,
among more and more blood.
So how will the sea amaze you when it arrives?
How will songs amaze you, or the butterfly,
or women's expensive perfumes, or their beautiful dresses,
or the rose that leans seductively against the wall
as a bird or a boy plucks it?
And with these countless deadly bayonets,
how will you number your wounds
so we may sing a little?

# Renovation

He renovates a tin window
to open it for the morning birds.
And renovates some stars that have burned out
in the streets, and a woman massacred in the neighborhood.
He renovates a memory demolished like a wall,
a bird's scattered ashes,
light reflected off a blade in the dark,
a woman lost in a spacious bed
and a bellow.
He renovates a friend's face as the sea breaks over it
and the singer who no longer resembles his songs,
the wind when it sleeps forgetting the immensity of an orbit,
the taste of words in conversation,
the taste of air and fruit
and two legs that have never carried a planet
while destruction prevails.
He renovates a womb, subdues horses
and poems that beg for livelihood in the shade
before slipping into a chicken coop or blowing by
like a steaming train.
He renovates pillars, neighs,
guns covered with moss from waiting.
He renovates a promise, roots, clouds,
and in the end he is slain alone like a lighthouse.

## A Beautiful Morning

A beautiful morning
is one that passes and I am not killed.
A city street following the sun at sunset
is obstructed by a roadblock and soldiers.
Another street runs after her
and never returns.

A beautiful morning…

≈ ≈ ≈

On the road I embrace an old woman's sadness
and woo her.
Yesterday laughs inside her
as she whispers: *Am I still youthful?*
Then she smiles and prays for me.

≈ ≈ ≈

I ruffle the hair of a small boy selling newspapers
and ask: *Anything new?*
Like every other morning he hands me
the chronicles of thirty years and a thousand moons.
He argues with me, then goes away shouting:
*Newspapers.*
The inspectors kill him,
but it is his habit to return to the streets
selling newspapers the following morning.

A beautiful morning…

≈ ≈ ≈

At the abyss of long waiting
I slip into a restaurant on a side street
and turn my eyes to the faces of passersby
and as I lean back in my metal chair
the fear of her not showing up gnaws at me.
With my last bite of bread
she surprises me briefly
in the face of an excited young woman,
but I realize the difference between them.
At the abyss of waiting
the road branches out in my body
and traffic lights blink on and off.
Many people cross
but no one is here.

≈ ≈ ≈

Her sorrow makes her come at last
and like a flower she bids me good evening.
I say: *You are late.*
*—You know the wide streets are clogged with checkpoints.*
We walk together with her hand in mine.
She suffuses the pores of my flesh.
The street becomes noisy:
*Soldiers, soldiers!*
They surround me and shoot at my forehead,
then read out my rights!
I am left in her arms like a corpse on an open road.

A beautiful morning...

≈ ≈ ≈

Tomorrow, when the sun touches my forehead,
I will ruffle the hair of a young boy
and like every other morning he will hand me
the chronicles of thirty years and a thousand moons
and together we will sell his wares.
My beloved will pass by ...
to buy the daily paper from me.
She will ruffle my hair
and like the seasonal trees go to her appointment.

A beautiful morning...

# The Soldier

He scatters his belongings on the river bank:
neglected guns and trenches filled with sand and time.
He looks all around,
takes off his uniform with decorum,
sits on top of the rocks in his tattered white underwear,
sinks his feet into the foam of boredom
and sings, with composure, a song.

≈ ≈ ≈

Midday passes before his eyes.
He fails to see the sun.
He takes a stone and throws it into the water
and watches the circles widen.

Midday passes before his eyes.
He fails to see the blood in the river.
He takes up a knife and throws it into the water
and watches the circles widen.

Midday passes before his eyes.
Night takes him by surprise.
He throws his rifle into the water.
The circles hurry to the banks.
He is surrounded by eyes that peer from balconies of blood
and silent graves.

# The Celebration

Flowers, songs, chants...
A memory from antiquity...
Saturday's dawning sun...
An orphan is late...
A widow comes by embracing another widow...
A singer...
Verses from the *Qur'an* ...
A flute on the outskirts of a neglected village...
Ancient soldiers...
Battles, defeated ages...
Thirty wars announced by daylight...
Another thirty still hidden in their sheaths...
Little ones dressed up for a feast...
Horses filled with the joy of their riders...
A procession coming from far away...
Ululations reaching the sky, a commotion...
Men emerging from darkness...
from yesterday's newspapers, from the inkwell.
All of them came,
took pictures,
cursed the end of life and memory,
drank from the cup of a slain dream,
before their leader stepped forward
to cut the silk ribbon
and open the graveyard.

# The Guide

The soul rises from bedrock to the earth's surface.
The sun's shadow lengthens like a tall tree
and calls out for help from a balcony
as the sun goes down like
a fallen foal or a slain crescent.

≈ ≈ ≈

A desert.

≈ ≈ ≈

Seas of sand were soaked up by mirages in the east
and in the west they evaporated in the wind.
We searched for a star,
but, growing pale, he asked us which way
we were going.

≈ ≈ ≈

Seven men, three women and a child...
We were carrying a few things in our hands.
He said: *This way,*
so we followed him
Then he said: *I am hungry* ...
We gave him our food and as he rested,
like a grove of palm trees, we shaded him.

≈ ≈ ≈

The wind heats the stars at midday,
the earth beneath us becomes ashes
while the sun above us blazes
with mythic blades
and the shifting embers of molten metals.

≈ ≈ ≈

For a whole year grass sprouted from our flesh,
then became dry.
A dream ripened and the neigh of a horse was lost.
There wasn't even a small stone to sleep on.

≈ ≈ ≈

Rest a little on my body.
I am the ruins that flow with your love.

≈ ≈ ≈

Not one of us collapsed
or cried out because the path was long.

≈ ≈ ≈

He lit up the dark with his singing:
*It is I who turns over the wilderness like my own palm,*
*reaching out to steal a star from the skies,*
and he brushes away the night from his face, singing:
*O Beauty*

≈ ≈ ≈

We followed him.
He said: *I am hungry.*
So we gathered in counsel
and then slaughtered one among us,
Six men…
three women…
and a child.
A day of lamentations,
a night … two nights—
then he fell down
and said: *I am hungry.*
We slaughtered a woman.
He said: *I am hungry.*
He gazed at the child:
*I will eat him before his clay decomposes and he grows thin.*
We followed him.

≈ ≈ ≈

Only two of us remained.
He said: *I will spare you so you can follow me*
*and witness our arrival*
*and the journey's end.*
We walked on, but he said: *I am hungry.*
He turned toward me in excitement
and stepped over my frail shadow.

≈ ≈ ≈

In the end no one arrived
but the guide!

## The Survivors

They were here for a year at our doorstep,
sleepless with their brown flesh-and-blood complexions,
knocking against our ribs to make us see them.
At the end of the night they depart.
They circle around the city seven times
like the revolving sun,
like a reverberating echo.
They kill the silence with their flutes
and light and birds hover around them
as they swim in the shadows
of tall wheat spikes and white stags.
As night falls the wind shakes the streets
and the darkness breathes out crazed spears among trees
jostling toward the windows and balconies.
We heard the hooves of their horses,
so we hid in the corners,
under beds, between ribs.
We hid like a storm among branches.
Their olives will eventually grow tired …we said:
*It might snow …*
*soldiers might come by this evening and immediately kill them,*
*or like a sun's fading wish they might grow tired*
*and kill themselves.*
Night falls once more …the wind blows.
We hold our breath and retreat.
Boundless fear binds our hands … and our beating hearts.
The most recent among us said … Let us all rise and ask them:
*You who have been sleepless at our doorstep for a year*

*and two nights:*

*What do you want?*
Storms of corpses rushed to the corners.
The smell of death rose from the roofs of mirrors,
from the colors of the eyes.
*Let us all rise...* the most recent among us said.
And when we reached the door, they shouted at us:
*You... O dead ones...don't open the door!*

## The Visitor

He advances on tiptoe in the dark.
I recognize him.
Panting breaths rise on the dwindling pathways.
Frail stars fall from the sky.
Time, like water, is without color.

He advances in rustling white, passersby cannot see him
falling like tears and fading away
without words to tell what's inside his blueness.
His voice, like water, is without color.

He advances, stumbling.
He rises up, then stumbles again
like in a dream where rivers rise in the middle of a desert
                                        on mountain tops
and the wind, like water, is without color.

He chants a song of which I remember nothing
but the blood shed on paraffin streets
and a white memory,
and silence, like water, without color.

He raises a fist
to strike at my remnants scattered on doorsteps,
but sees me in them.
He retreats ten green steps
and throws light over the living who wake the night.
In all innocence the things around me ask:
*Who goes there?*

Name?
Like water, without color

## Possibilities

Maybe silence has grapes for a tongue
and flows inside us
and spreads us out like colored garments.

≈ ≈ ≈

Maybe the dust under siege
in our flesh is a marble horizon
to which birds have long prayed—
but it has never responded.

≈ ≈ ≈

Maybe fire's ancient sorrow is ashes
that torture it with our annihilation,
then leave it to moan.

≈ ≈ ≈

Maybe when water yearned for fire
it invented waves
so one day they might become flames.

≈ ≈ ≈

Maybe love thrives in our bodies' innocence,
in the mixing of the seasons and our vital organs,
in shadows that pull at our ears in gentle reproof.

≈ ≈ ≈

Maybe the sea, too, dreams like us
of living by the sea
and falling in love.

≈ ≈ ≈

Maybe our feet
conceal our travels
toward old secrets
we could not reach
because the road became tired.

≈ ≈ ≈

Maybe I know the whole story
but hide part of it from myself
to love the story more.

## The Foal

It flares like a comet, as if the tumultuous ground were a cloud
and the prairies were on fire,
bidding farewell to stones and scribbling on silence with thunder.
It was as kind as the appearance of the sun,
full of love and the virgin joy in its breast.
It does not move away to avoid the arrow, it does not falter
like a bird that has departed too hastily into the night,
forgetting its wings when it sees
what the spreading dark and eyes have failed to see,
after it has seen an earth as wide as madness
and a wish that has conquered time.
It has its land, hills of neighing, eyes,
and is what we wish to be,
for it is the sharpest of swords,
the most faithful refuge and friend,
and the highest battlement.

# The Stairs

There you ascend and descend,
leaving a window in my heart.
You surprise my sleep and steal it,
ascending, descending—then you go away like an
                                       intemperate gazelle.
I am tired:  Won't you stop so I can pick up a stone or stick
and remove the minutes from my body
and the pain of the years from the dust
in the yawning distance?
So I can brush away the weariness of years,
the dew as it breaks,
and the butterflies of longing?

There you ascend and descend,
amid the silence of the pine
and the shiver of steps as they search
for a home, a room, or the neighing of a horse.
You are much more tired than I ...
but beautiful.
Your strides are shorter than mine ...
but you are tall.
So don't end up like my shadow.
You are closer to me than my songs
and when I gather my heart to contain you
you become departure itself.

There you ascend and descend.
A dream still surrounds you—
and the classrooms, theaters, walls, flowers,

and the shadows of embers.
Even excitement still surrounds you.

The pine is green.
The grass is green.
From one day to the next the shadows of buildings
grow and grow as they
share the sun and the stairs with us.
But between us nothing has changed.

There is a window as high as our hands can reach.
For six years it remained cold, dark, and closed,
but between us nothing has changed.
There you ascend,
descend,
ascend,
descend,
and grief becomes greater
and greater...and greater.

# The Chairs

- **End**

Our ribs break loose like the chairs
from which
we watch the sea at sunset
Isolation embitters the day
A bold grief lies behind our smile
Being with people implies escape
Our legs sink into the dust like chairs
left in a garden after war

## • Intermission

The chairs don't remember
They sit here like we do
and count the leaves
of this generous autumn
When the count reaches forty
the wind comes from all directions
spurning us and dying away
But the chairs don't remember
They sit here resting like we do

## • **Strangers**

How dark how dull
Those who came and went away like strangers
Even their women and small girls were sullen
This is how the chairs sit quietly thinking
in the evening

## • End (2)

Darkness and different ages have passed over
the stone chairs that sank into the ground
long ago
Many kings and emperors made thrones of them
Appointed with silk and clouds of perfume
It seemed then that the wheel would no longer go round
Now they dream of people and scream cry howl and bellow
If only once they could see the sun
If only once they could smell the birds' droppings

## • **Parting**

A chair in the garden in the cold and dark
Thick silence descends on the place
On the bewildered moment
A couple was here five minutes ago
They talked a lot
and have left nothing behind on the chair
but a feeling of coldness
and the lament of a wilting carnation

## • Tumult

At the end of the day
when people leave their places in the garden
where illusion has an illusion it calls reality
the chairs wake up and drag their stiff legs
through passageways now faint beneath the moon
They start a long playful scene
by scaring the trees in the dark
They imitate the voices of those who left behind
silence sadness stories and sullen laughter
Who look as if their souls had never been touched
by a single drop of rain
Longer and longer becomes the night
And in the morning the chairs resume the silence of stone
Danger danger
A bird spots some people far off at the garden gate

- **Sorrows**

It had been abandoned among the forgotten table
and the darkness and silent walls and dim corners
Then came those from a faraway land brutalized
                                    by forgetfulness
They ate drank laughed
and adjusted their legs under the heedless table
In a moment of complete of intoxication wine spilled
from a woman's cup and the chair cried out
*How thirsty I am*
and drank of her wine, her laughter
and cupped her bottom—it beguiled her
and slipped away toward the gate
staggering drunk in Amman's darkness

## • Black Longing

The chair shares fears with the little one:
The stab of the wind
The extreme of December loneliness
The fire of the summer's hearth
The cane
His school grades
The dread of a question
A dry throat
It shares his boredom in class over every letter
tricked by the neigh in a hymn
and by a sentence at the mercy of one character
The little one beseeched God for seven years
to urge him to go to school
to explore the seas of the sunlit globe
The little one tortured by the wind
and the stakes of his wretched tent
dreamed of a wooden chair in the corner of the classroom
protected by a ceiling
on which to doze a little every day

## • **Occupation**

A seat wandering with the people on a bus
throbs as my heart does
when a stunning woman spurns the other seats
and comes over to sit down

## • Trick

The seat in the cinema
cheered joyfully for the hero
Happy in the dark
Happy that metal had once more been vanquished
O, if only it could reach the doorstep
to see how often they slaughter a martyr
in the broad light of day

## • Conspiracy

A chair invites me to rest my unrestrained feet
so it might walk in my place
and know the feel of racing with the wind

## • Death

When we depart the chairs will laugh
confident they have our consent
And they will follow us to see us silent in bed
or at the table

## • **Warning**

Be careful!
Some chairs dislike heavy words or poems that cling
and after a little while they might cast those
who sit on top of their hearts
to the very end of Hell

- **Chairs**

Chairs will distract us in war
Overwhelm us in peace
and forgive us like sins
Chair Hell
Chair Intercession
And whenever something new appears
they shout
*Die—so courage can live*
They dearly love people
People's contentment
Though chairs made of blood on top of blood
cannot withstand the bloom of a dream
As those chairs were never trees

# The Hours

**The Clock**

It draws us as its hands go round,
stealing what it desires from our lives,
and returns to count up its spoils in the caves of the night.
As it opens its second hand
it startles at an empty palm:
*Have I ... have I stolen only dust?*

## Three in the morning

A morning cloud and shy lightning.
Islands of visions and birds singing.
Shade trees.
Alert statues.
A sword held up to the sheath of darkness
to draw out into the universe the dawning of the ages.

**Four in the morning**

A wing brushes the face of a sleeping female.
Beaks melt in fires of song in the branches.
Pebbles blossom among the footsteps of martyrs
coming home to mother.

**Six in the morning**

The earth's midwife,
Doomsday Bridge
between dew and braids,
between the expanse and the eruption of life.
Appointments at the extreme of greenness
and the alleyways' message
for the open paths.

**Twelve noon**

A mother tries in vain to tidy up
the unruly boys' turmoil.
When the air becomes heavy, fire acquires wings
and the dust of this wreckage anticipates
an urn of dreams and a drop of water!

### Two in the afternoon

The wolf's siesta.
The fox's den.
A blade of secret fire cuts into the neck of the water.
Countries are laden with victims
and stalled by tyrants' spears.

**Five in the evening**

The jasmine returns home safely.
Bright shadows shiver in a spacious square.
Trees feign youth while watching a full-breasted woman
and try to imitate her voluptuous figure!

**Seven in the evening**

A boring family biography:
The appearance of the broadcaster
as we sit obediently in a prison of programs.
Our pulse drowses while yearning
or rain
beats against our windows.

**Eight in the evening**

Our porcelain days sway
with the voice of the clown—the broadcaster.
A scene of a huge massacre,
of fear,
but he, as is his custom,
reads on, smiling for everyone.

## Eleven at night

Books for bringing on sleep,
a drizzle of sleep.
The little ones go on a daring hunt for dream-horses
and the lusty wind invades sails
and pounds the ships.
Fidgeting in a nearby bed
a woman yawns:
*I am tired of this day, Hassan!*

## Twelve midnight

The midnight hour
catches us asleep
and carelessly slaughters us ...
We try to fool it by rehearsing a day,
having a doze,
then a long sleep.
But it slaughters us once more
and whispers while contemplating
its victims: *How familiar they look!*

**The hour of birth**

A crazy awakening
has languished in my blood for a thousand years.
It disturbs the dust
to become a desert
or a carnation.

## The hour of death

It vanquishes the openness that rides with the wind
and attacks, freeing me of my question.
And as I doze as the time of my departure draws near
it introduces me to my shadows.

**The hour of love**

For twenty years
I took the same path
and crossed with this crowd.
But suddenly many roses appear on the balconies
and everywhere I go
my body is touched by dew
and doves rush toward me.

## The hour of the despot

It will brush away what remains of dust
to see us more clearly
and laugh like a content wolf
when it sees that we have lost
the most beautiful among us.

## The hour of nightmare

I creep toward absence
carrying the tired earth on my shoulders.
But my blood stirs
and I wake from sleep like a stone
with a bitter body
and veins of wood.

## The hour of arrest

Usually, a solitary gazelle prepares songs for its young
and at dawn lullabies the question's wound.
But suddenly they cross the streets—in great numbers—
and a woman asks:
What are they doing with those guns?
Have they come to arrest the mountains?

## The hour of execution

Silently, soldiers go round in the barracks
and famished dogs rush out.
There are the monotonous sounds of footsteps
in chains
and in darkness.
Silently, a knotted rope swings
in a rush of bullets and death.

**The twenty fifth hour**

Nothing can catch it,
not advancing time or chains
or the security forces,
as it dwells in us like a ravenous spring
in full view
in our light and tender songs.

## Eight in the morning

I fold up the poem and get up
before bringing the birds to completion.
It is time for work
and now my soul is dark
but my necktie is clean!

# Mirrors of Dust

## Shadows

Our souls have become shadows in the dust,
so who will circle around us
after they leave?
Who will visit us on a pilgrimage
so we can renew time in all places?
Shadows might have shadows:
Them … us…
you…and you…
and me.

## Treasures

Time holds the fractured treasures of the dust:
Minutes cast off from childhood thrones,
drizzles on an ocean of moments and delirious footsteps,
years spilled on old pages,
an epoch chased by a forest of canes,
and the distant rhythm of a dance on the oak's corpse.
There are treasures in the dust
dreaming of our roaming bodies
and of a void.

## Father

Father lies in the dust,
his voice trembles in prayer, his fingers sow,
he is hidden, but he recognizes us by our desiccated wheat:
*Those are my footsteps and you have some of my features.*
He will recognize us by our bitter homelessness at home,
our absence from ourselves,
by our name being Kamal.
We will weep as mother beats us.
She will not believe that father is here
when we run and point to the handful of dust behind us.
She will not believe that father is here.
Father is here!

## Deserts

There are deserts in the dust
causing heartache in exile.
A river becomes confused by its grasses
and forgets me and war blazes
in the laughter of the last day.
My soul's other
forgets the promises I made to the sea
and the flowers of my confessions.
In the dust there are deserts
longing to forget my greenness
and the mint of my shadow
on the doorsteps.
They only remember me—
when those who've gone far away are remembered—
by the dryness of my fever.

## Brother

I have a brother in the dust
who has been waiting for thirty years for his toys.
How did we not wait for him, he will ask us.
How did age take us by surprise?
How did we grow up?
And how is it, just like that, we've never invited him to join us?
Not once did we invite him
into our games in the mirror, in our dreams,
just like that!
One of our games is:
We have a brother in the dust.
When winter comes he waves with the grass.
He beguiles us with intense whiteness—that's his habit—
then dwells close to our father, over there, inside mother.

## Signs

There are signs hidden in the dust
that dislike this place.
They worship the wind that scatters them
across the morning valley
and in exploding gardens
and onto the back of a hymn
or a horse.
And when they stumble upon us
they trip over their own feet,
as time slips by.

≈ ≈ ≈

Tell me O Age ... my killer,
how much have you conquered the heart?
How much poplar and balsam must you have
before we can be scattered once more
into that abyss of delirium
where the things we are known by
are lost?

## Tents

There are tents of blood and terror
in the dust
pitched there to make a myth of the sky.
There are tents of wind in our blood
that take us everywhere though we appear motionless,
so the lime in the lore of the *mejana*
and a smell from the sea surround us.
The singer has multiplied in us.
The Imam has multiplied in us.
The broadcaster has multiplied in us.
Talk has multiplied in us.
Departure and the medallions of war multiply and
fragment our bodies with victory!
And we are still here,
fifty years old—steeped in killing—
and on our own.

## Fingers

There are fingers of cane in the dust
that touch the songs in our hearts,
torturing us for a thousand years to make us roam
so they, having memorized the lands of the wind,
might follow our footsteps
and our dreams of women.
When the fingers tighten on the flute with desire
we realize the secret of the springs inside us
and cry out: *O land of all reptiles,*
*Don't...*
*Don't...*
*Don't remember us!*

## An Arm

There is an arm in the dust
and an unfinished waist in clay.
We will visit fifty songs
and countries that look out on a thousand seas
to see them filled with hope.
We will urge the wide expanse to stray with us,
then beguile it.
We will step inside its magic, chanting:
*Blaze, O myths.*
We might have an arm in the dust,
perhaps we'll dream it in the dream of a waist
that will one day be ours.

## Talk

There is a lot of talk in the dust
about the house, the sea,
and the faraway balconies.
It escapes the ink
so we won't see our gardens
set in the newspaper's frost.
We will chant aloud
the words that will take us wherever the poem
wishes us to go and we will sing them
when we meet our slayer.

## Birds

There are birds in the dust
that purify the poems of our sorrow,
that return us to our childhood names
and copybooks.
They watch us love this place
and our cages.
There are birds in the dust
that in the end will come into our traps
but will not taunt us
with the chains around our souls.

## Windows

There are windows in the dust
that coax the river out of its lament
for a morning conversation, for wild thyme,
for thresholds that disappear with our steps.
With a few roses they ignite the horizon
inviting spacious plains and hills to our courtyard,
releasing in us the yearnings of young girls for horses.
They lay us open and wonder about us,
becoming watchful when a mother's voice is absent
and half of our stories have gone astray.
When night falls we remove their curtains with stealth
so their light might show us the way back home...

## Countries

There are villages and towns in the dust
amid heaps of ashes.
Now time has scattered them,
their suns and their names dispelled.
There are towers without guards in the dust,
paths without people,
blunt swords searching for sharpness,
a reason for every absence and return.
There are countries buried in the dust.
So the wind went to the wilderness
to speak of their lore to the silence.

## A Companion

We had a companion in the dust
we quietly got used to, but he left us
to drift in the sands of our souls,
in what remains of our speech and
our cautionary songs
that pass with the morning.
But when we came to live here,
our companion who loves to migrate with the dust
was killed.

## A Bed

In the dust there's a bed of whiteness
from which to look upon
our relatives' prayers,
and a flute,
supplications,
flowers of bitterness,
a silence that foretells startled trees in darkness,
and a wasteland reserved for graves
so that the stones are not wasted.
In the dust there's a bed of yearning for our roots
and our losses.
There's a universe that will arise
in the morning—made graceful by the living—
to conceal its violence in the dust.

## Commandments

There are commandments in the dust
that shine on our dreams and guard us.
They guide the jasmine back to itself
when it doesn't know us.
There are commandments surrounding us in the dust:
a verse for the clouds,
a verse to bemoan the heavy silence
and the genesis of bridles,
and a verse that does not sleep,
that follows us into death.
There are commandments in the dust
that will keep tormenting us
until we conquer this darkness
with dreams.

## Branches

There are branches in the dust,
familiar as shadows.
They are the stalks of old age—
and balconies that overlook the soul and the valleys,
and a greenness opposing a dry day,
and dancing and singing.
They share their light with us
and we share all we have with them.

≈ ≈ ≈

Every olive we plant
plants us, close by, over there.

## Roofs

We will raise our roof high on the road in the dust,
away from advancing armies
and from the desires of moles and in dens,
away from the slain who accepts his slayer as his guard
and from the carnation that quivers
in the collar of a despot.
We will raise our roof high in the dust
and when the weight of time is pressed upon us
we will bend down
and it will stay up high.

## Languages

A scream echoes in the dust.
Before words had time to divide in our bodies
they got lost among estranged nations
and our prayers were dispersed.
Half of them swelled from knowing
the honey of love,
in love and in song.
There is an intimate conversation in the dust
about a cave and clouds,
the youthful passion of plants,
our souls incarnated as tigers,
and our yearning for girls.
But blood bursts with life
leaving behind all these languages!

## Taste

There's the dewy taste of seas and clouds in the dust,
the taste of the expanse and the rain,
of plains, mountains, humans,
of femininity, love, and intrepid oranges,
of childhood and saffron,
of living in my mother's heart,
of travel,
and of your soul and mine.
But my beloved trees steal toward the source
to taste it in solitude, before any of us.

## Lungs

There are lungs in the dust.
Are we the air they breathe when they pant
as we echo in them?
They run on so the grass can heal inside us,
so we can resurrect them from nothingness.
The lungs in the dust are shadowed by fear.
They recount the fall of loved ones
full of regret when their souls ascend,
when …
There are lungs in the dust
that find air in clouds and in songs
but they gasp, my friend, each time
blood is shed on the earth.

## Playgrounds

There are playgrounds in the dust held by the madness
our little ones have for their games.
There are shores that slip through their dreams
and their fingers
as we grow tired.
They have a fragile castle to guard
and a tiger that in the end resembles a rabbit!
My dear old friend in galloping horses and in oaks,
my dear old friend in every grain of salt and every planet,
are you a tiger?
Or a castle that will come apart in the hands of the little ones
when the wind at the horizon is a claw?
How loudly I call out.  Do the clouds hear me?
O clouds, don't imprison the water, for the dust here is suffering.
My dear old friend and twin on horseback,
why do I see you in the sand?
Which handful of sand are you?
For sand has become a playground for sand...

## Horses

We might have horses in the dust
that will examine the earth and the horizon in us.
They'll depart if the stairs of blood
do not collapse into light, color and meaning.
Horses that will behold the morning in us and run to it,
that will carry lightning words to their source
and the singer home with his flute in his hands.
We will whisper: *We have arrived.*
And they will neigh: *No, we have not.*
We'll reach nothing upon our arrival.
We'll reach nothing upon our arrival...

## CURBSTONE PRESS, INC.

is a nonprofit publishing house dedicated to multicultural litera-
ture that reflects a commitment to social awareness and change,
with an emphasis on contemporary writing from Latino, Latin
American, and Vietnamese cultures.

Curbstone's mission focuses on publishing creative writers whose
work promotes human rights and intercultural understanding, and
on bringing these writers and the issues they illuminate into the
community. Curbstone builds bridges between its writers and the
public—from inner-city to rural areas, colleges to cultural centers,
children to adults, with a particular interest in underfunded public
schools. This involves enriching school curricula, reaching out
to underserved audiences by donating books and conducting
readings and educational programs, and promoting discussion in
the media. It is only through these combined efforts that literature
can truly make a difference.

Curbstone Press, like all non-profit presses, relies heavily on the
support of individuals, foundations, and government agencies
to bring you, the reader, works of literary merit and social
significance that would likely not find a place in profit-driven
publishing channels, and to bring these authors and their books
into communities across the country.

If you wish to become a supporter of a specific book—one that
is already published or one that is about to be published—your
contribution will support not only the book's publication but also
its continuation through reprints.

We invite you to support Curbstone's efforts to present the diverse
voices and views that make our culture richer, and to bring these
writers into schools and public places across the country.
Tax-deductible donations can be made to:
Curbstone Press, 321 Jackson Street, Willimantic, CT 06226
phone: (860) 423-5110  fax: (860) 423-9242
www.curbstone.org